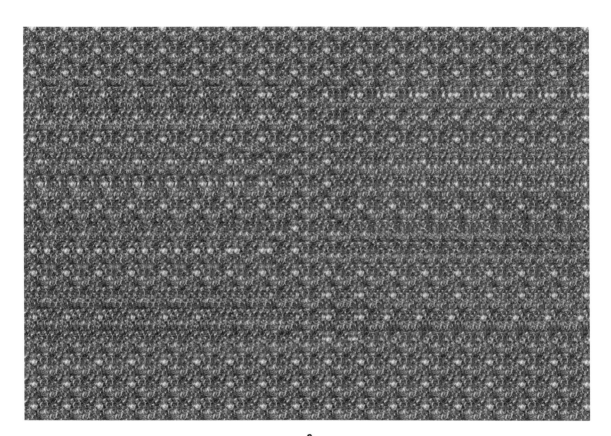

TAKE THAT BOOKS

Take That Books is an imprint of
Take That Ltd.
P.O.Box 200
Harrogate
HG1 4XB

Illustrated by Dirk Ransome and Mogul

10 9 8 7 6 5 4 3 2

ISBN 1-873668-90-2

Layout and typesetting by Take That Ltd., P.O.Box 200, Harrogate, HG1 4XB.

Printed and bound in Great Britain.

It started with a kiss...

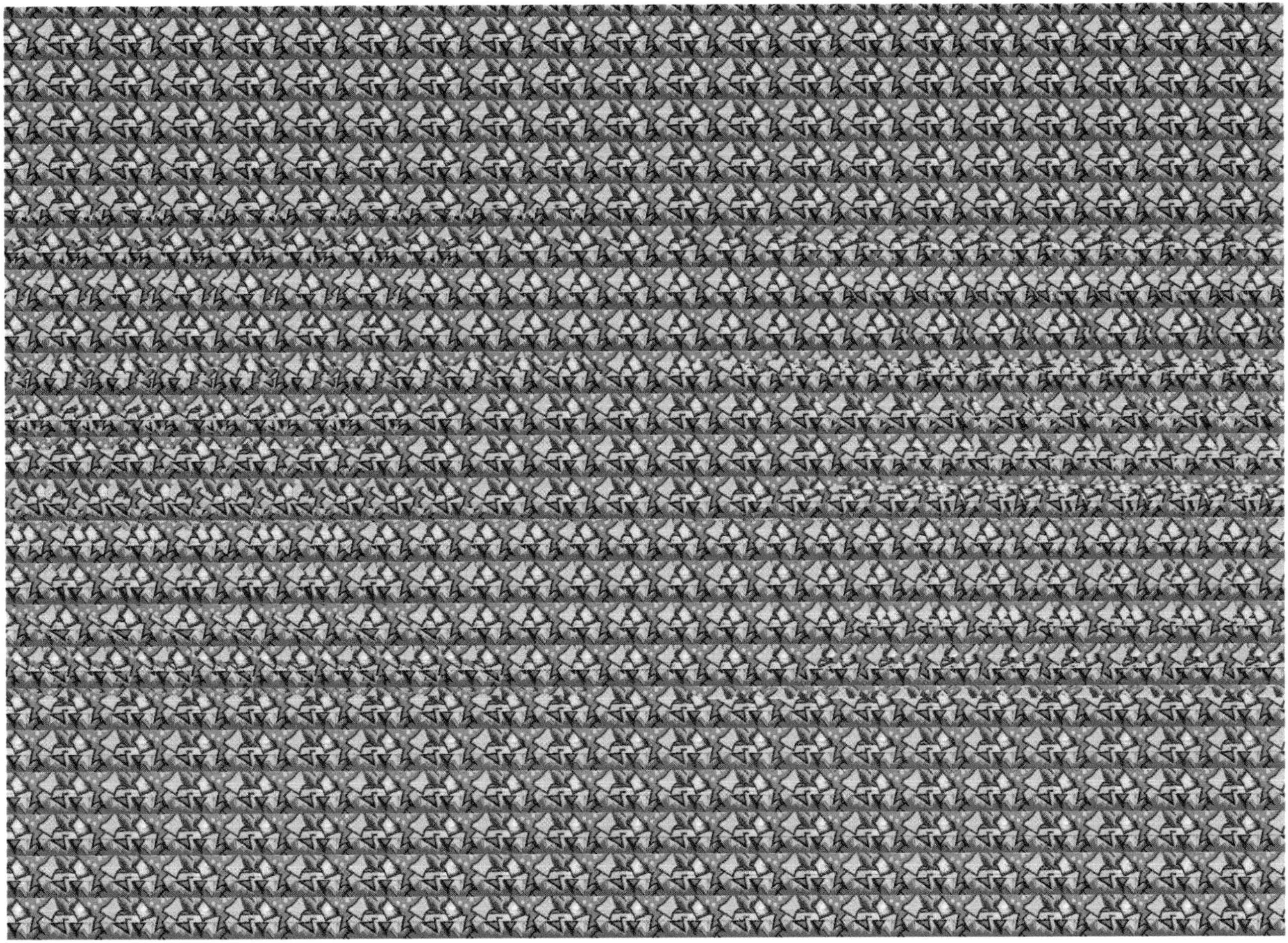

Suggestogram

This is the world's first thought invoked stereogram, which has been dubbed a Suggestogram™.

It works by transmitting heat from your hand into the contours of the image. Simply place your thumbs on the top corners of the stereogram as you think of your favourite subject, and the subject should appear within seconds.

A class of twelve year-olds were having a lesson on nourishment. Half way through the session the teacher asked a young boy to name four benefits of Mother's Milk.

"One," he replied, "it's nutritious. Two, it is fresh. Three, it is served at the right temperature. And four, it comes in a really delightful container!"

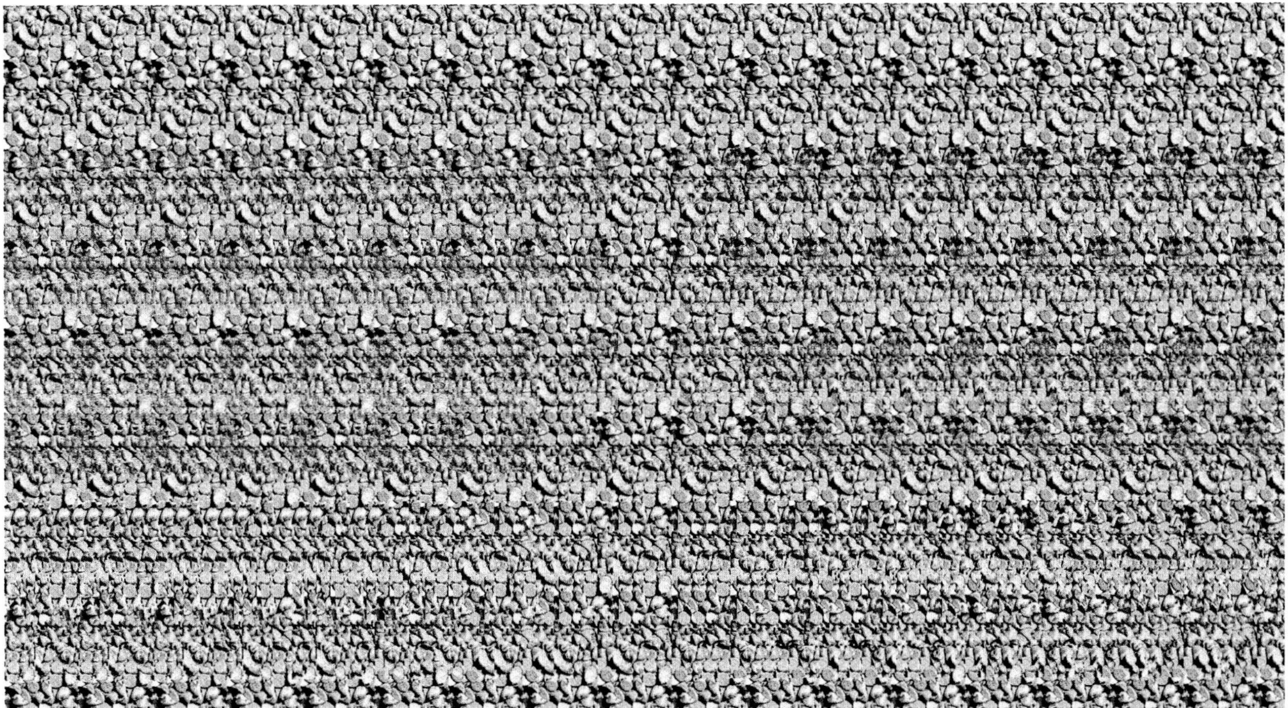

Lunchbox

Ever since Eve tempted Adam in the Garden of Eden, fruit has been associated with love and lust.

But what would you choose to put in your lunchbox?

Three nuns were walking along the road. The first described with her hands
the succulent grapefruits she had bought for the convent cocktail party.
The second described the enormous bananas she had bought, also using her hands.
The third nun, who was hard of hearing looked at both of them and asked,
"Brother who?"

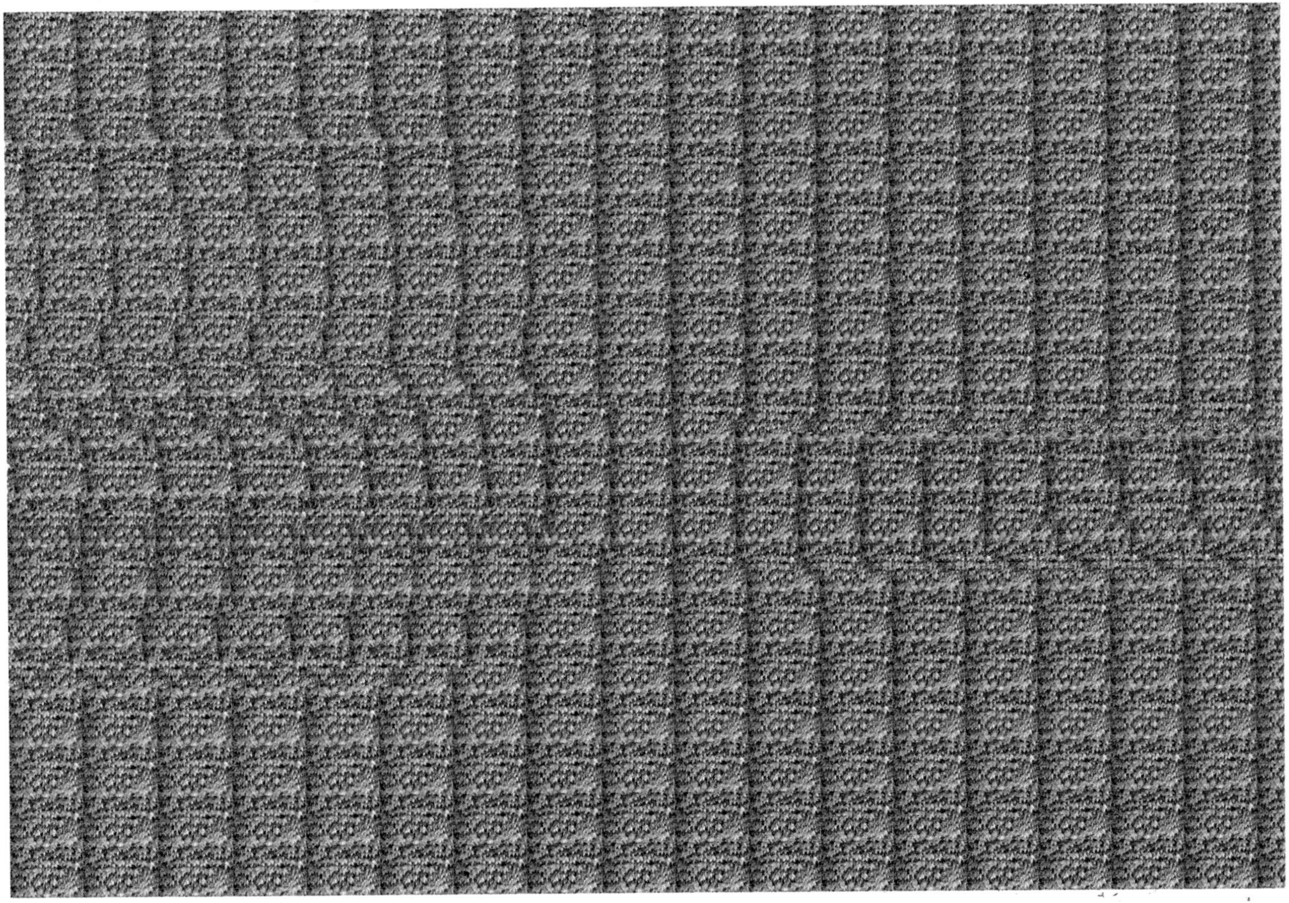

Standing room only

"Straight sex!"

"Straight sex!"

"I gave that up years ago. It's just the hard stuff for me!"

On their wedding night, Tracy went up to the bedroom to prepare herself. A few minutes later Sean arrived and knocked on the door. "Come on in Sean," giggled Tracy, "I'm not afraid." Sean paused for a couple of seconds and then replied, "You would be if you knew what I was knocking with!"

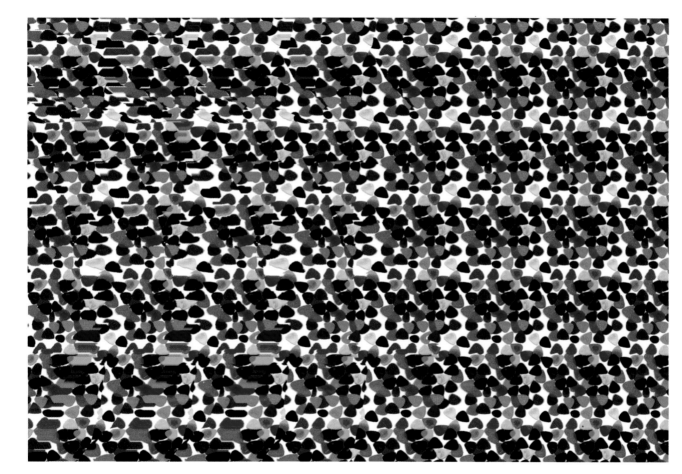

I Want Muscle

All that standing around can be tiring, so you'll be needing strong leg muscles. Here's one for the girls!

Times were hard, so James suggested to his wife Laura that they try a new way of saving money whilst having some fun. "Every time we make love I'll give you a pound for your housekeeping piggy bank" he suggested.

A few weeks later they decided to open the piggy bank.
Out tumbled some pound coins with loads of other assorted value notes.
"Laura, where did all this money come from?" he exclaimed.
"Do you think everyone is as stingy as you?" she replied.

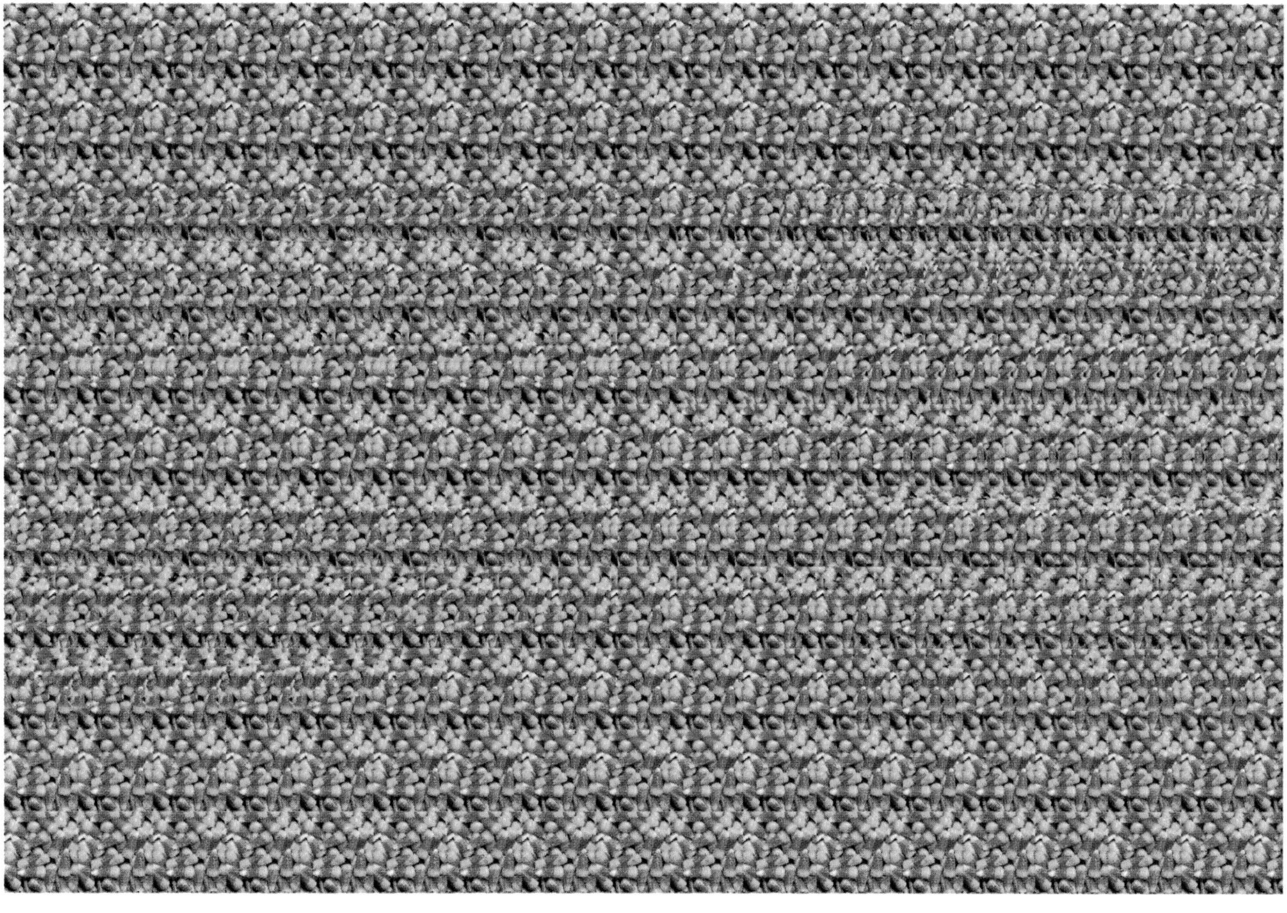

Glass Ceiling

Now the ladies are on a roll, perhaps that glass ceiling is in reach. Well don't stand on ceremony, get on up there - most men like a domineering woman.

A policeman came home early and found his wife in bed with his best friend.
"Hey, what do you think you're doing?" he asked.
"See. I told you he was stupid," the wife whispered to her lover.

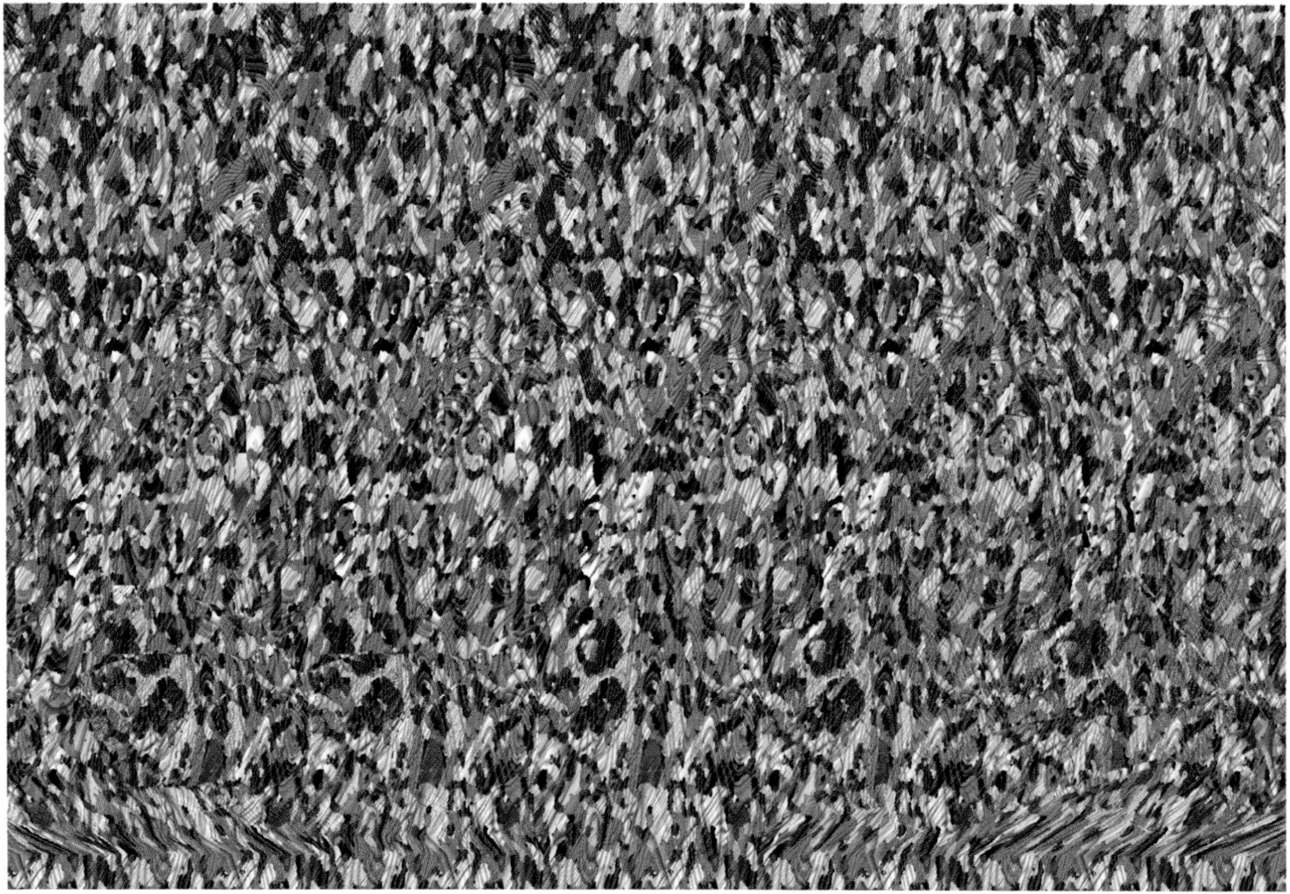

Come By

However, when faced with an aggressive woman, a lot of men will opt for something a little less threatening.

A famous millionaire was having a new house built on some land he had bought.

He told the architect, "Do not touch that tree as that is where I lost my virginity." "How sentimental," replied the architect. "And don't touch that tree over there either because that's where her mother stood watching". Flabbergasted the architect asked, "Her mother just stood there while you did it? But didn't she say anything?" "Yes - Baa," replied the millionaire.

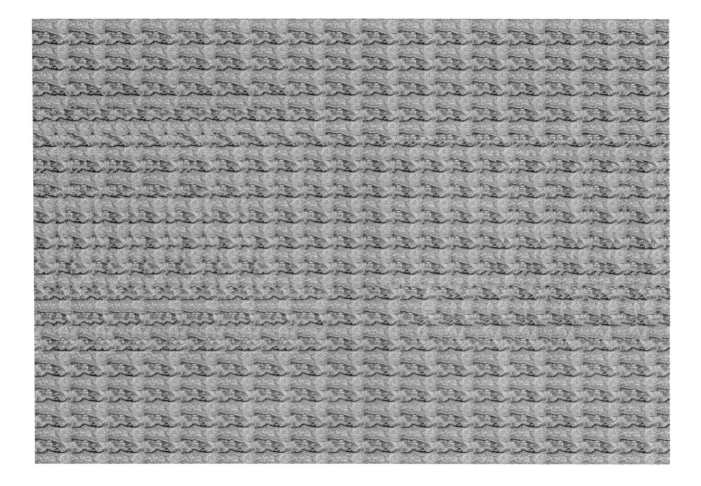

Silicone Valley

Bestiality is completely unnatural.
And so are these.

John left home early for a one week business trip to Germany. As he got to the end of the road he remembered he had left his airline tickets at home. He returned home and quietly entered the house.

To his surprise he saw his wife in a skimpy negligee doing the washing-up at the sink. He crept up behind her and gently tweaked her left breast.
"Just one pint today please," she said, "John's away this week".

What's it Worth?

Big breasts can cost an awful lot of money.
But there are ways of clawing back the investment.

Two ladies of the night were comparing notes in the massage parlour.
"The client I was with last night gave me two hundred quid"
"Gross?" asked the other.
"No, about six centimetres!"

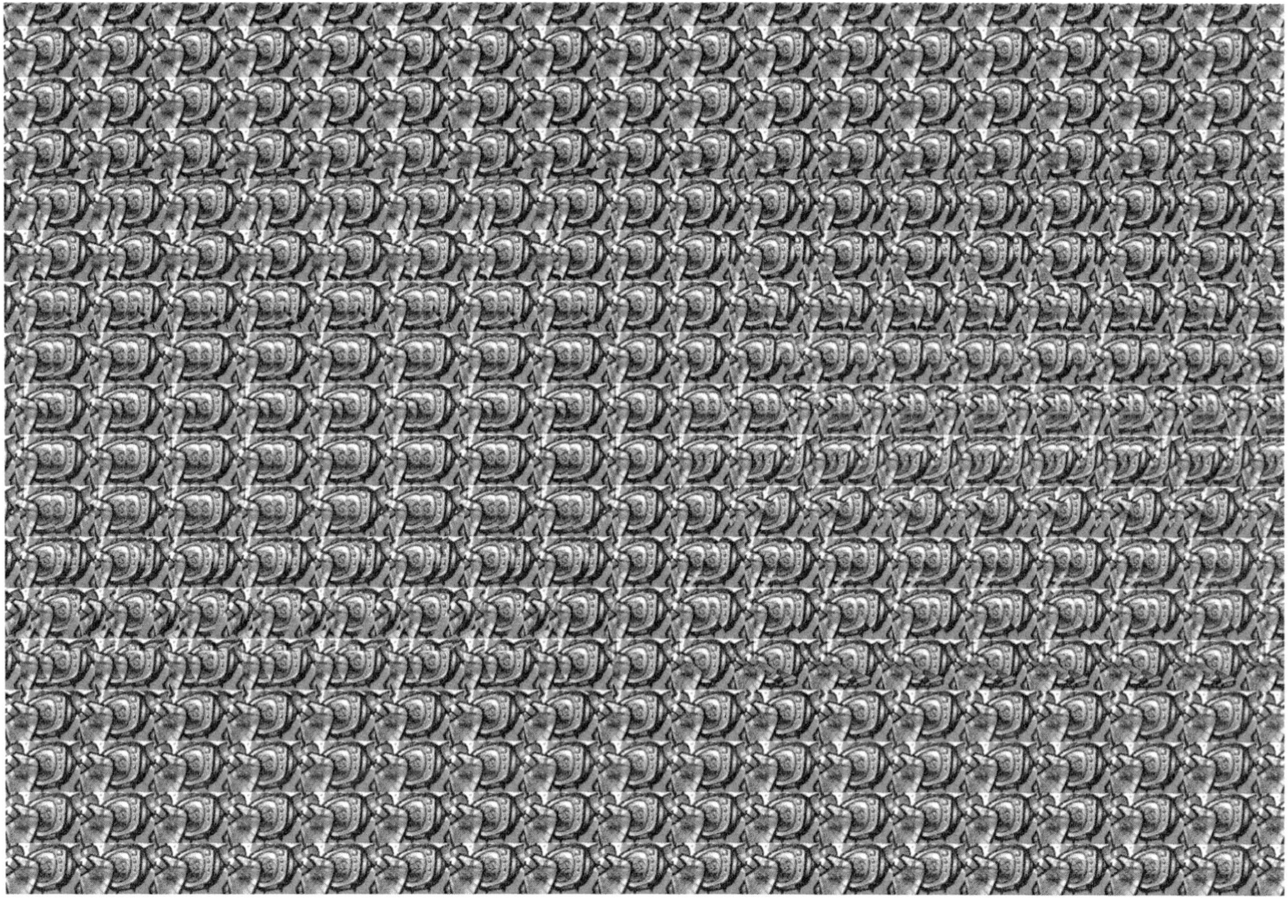

Implements

Having your back scratched at the right moment can heighten your pleasure.

But if you've a thick hide, it may take something more than long fingernails to bring you pain.

A young army major went along to his first high-society ball. He was in deep conversation with a beautiful young debutante when her necklace fell off and dropped down the back of her dress. The deb fluttered her eyelids and asked the major if he could help her get it. Slightly timidly he complied and placed his hand down the back of her dress. "I can't find it," he whispered. "Try further down," replied the deb. But as he pushed his hand down, he noticed a lot of the other guests were staring at him. "Oh dear," he said, "I feel a perfect ass". "Never mind that," complained the deb, "just get the necklace will you!"

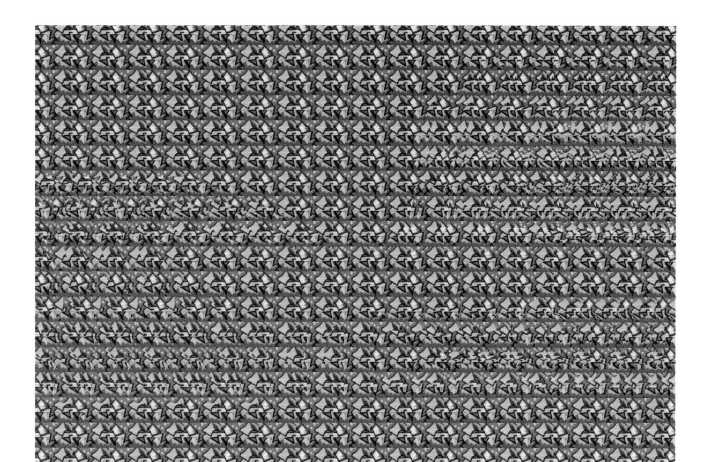

Bend Over

All of these activities really are very, very naughty.

What would your Mother say?

A sixteen year old girl was having a close relationship with her boyfriend and they decided to go the whole way. Not wanting to get pregnant she sensibly decided she would take precautions. The only problem was that she couldn't go to her doctor in case he told her mother.

So, she crept in to her mother's room one day and rummaged through the draws. Very soon she found her mum's pills and swapped them for some aspirin. All went well, the sex was great, and the girl didn't get pregnant. Unfortunately, her mum is expecting twins in February.

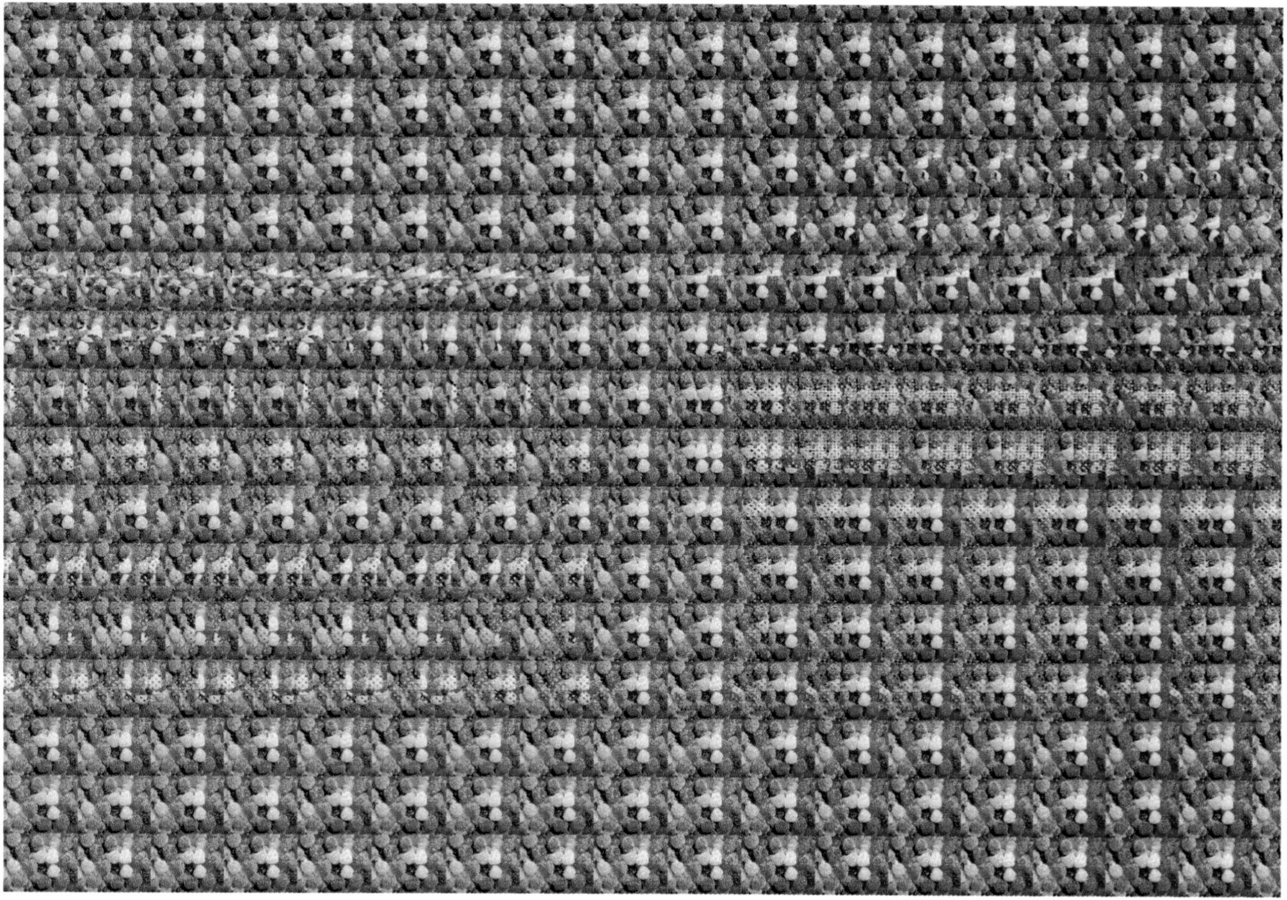

For Good Boys and Girls

If you are spanked for being naughty, then you should be rewarded if you are good.

Here's something for you to lick. And it should cool you down unless you put it in a strange place!

An old man was passing a playground one day when he spotted a sad looking youngster sat on the grass by himself crying his eyes out. Stooping down with a smile on his face, the old man asked the youngster what was wrong.

The little boy looked up into the friendly face and complained "I'm sad because I can't do what the big boys do." The old man promptly sat down next to the youngster and started crying his eyes out.

Was that a 99 or a 69?

Of course, once you've devoured your treat, your taste buds
may have been aroused.

Unless you are on a diet, you could try a bit of anything that
takes your fancy.

*A small boy got up in the middle of the night to go to the toilet. As he passed his
parents bedroom, he noticed the door was open and funny noises were coming from
within. He took a quick peek and saw his parents indulging in a bit of '69'.
Interrupting proceedings he admonished his mother, "I take it this means you won't
be taking me to the doctor on Monday because I've been sucking my thumb?"*

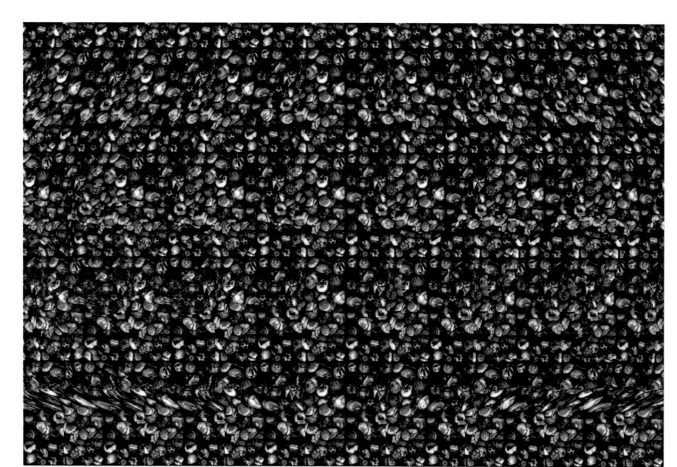

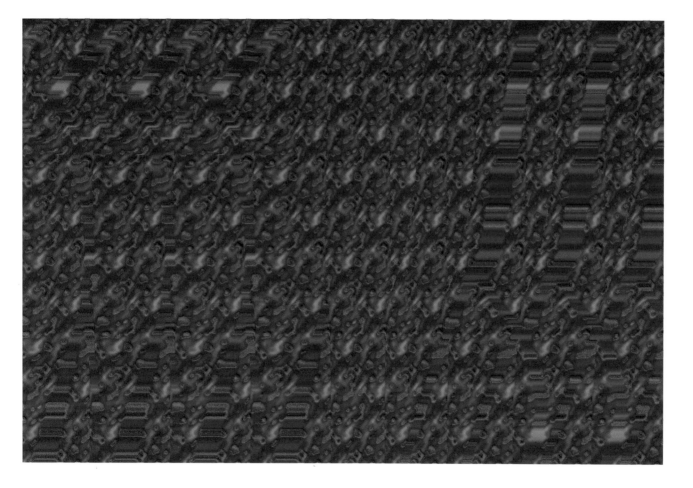

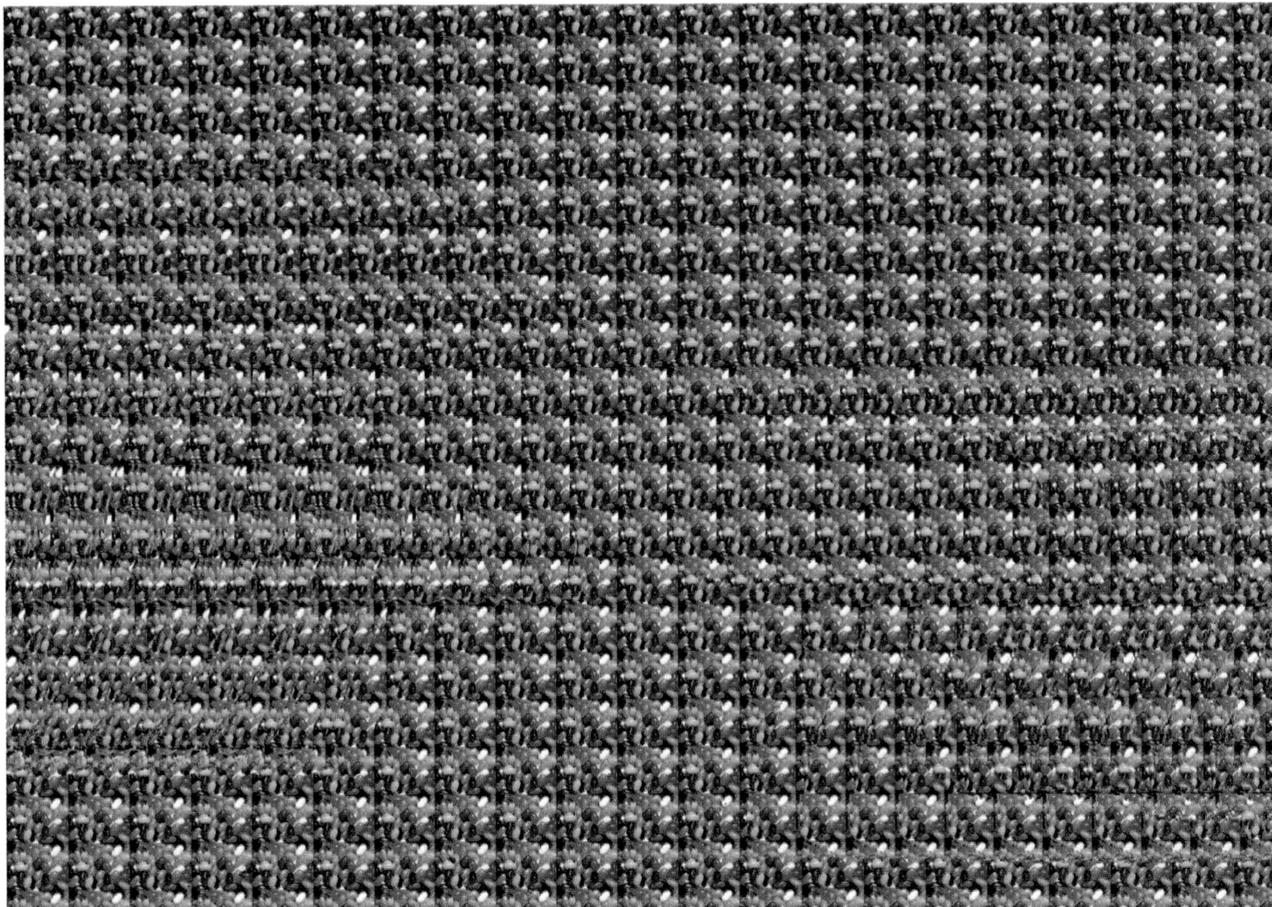

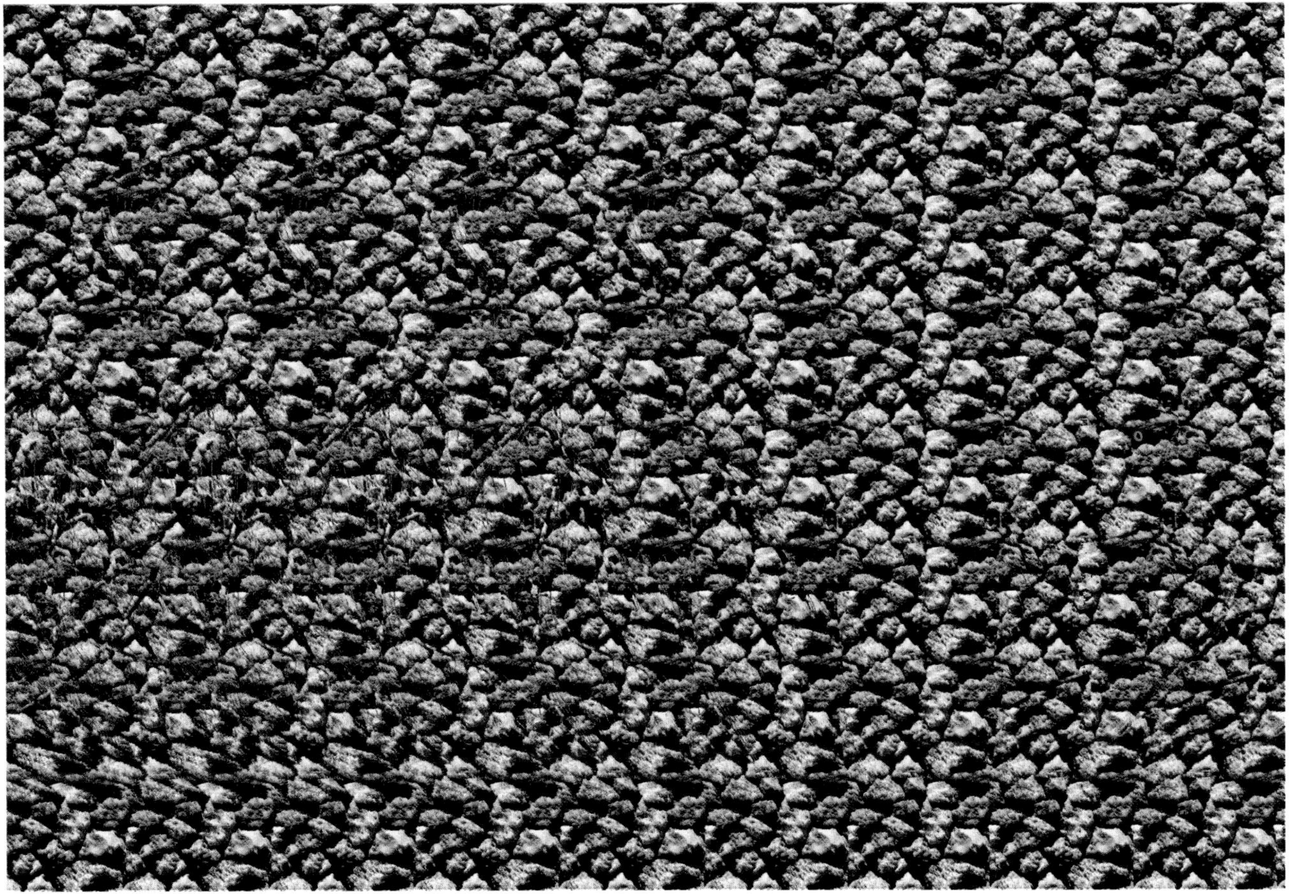

Blub Blub Blub

If you are prepared to get on your knees and beg for it, you may be amazed at the goodies which may come your way.

Sally was wearing a very tight skirt as it was summertime. When she tried to step up onto the bus she found she couldn't lift her leg high enough. She reached behind her and unzipped her zip. It did not seem to make any difference so she reached behind again to do it back up.

Suddenly the man behind her lifted her up high and carried her onto the bus.
"What the hell are you doing," she asked angrily.
"Well you unzipped my fly twice so I thought we were getting on pretty well".

Are you tired?

We are starting to get towards the rear of the book now, so you are probably becoming a little weary.

Try crawling into bed for a rest - or something else!

A man returned early from work to find his wife scrubbing the kitchen floor. The rhythmic movement of her body over the tiles gave him uncontrollable sensual ideas. Dropping his trousers, he lifted his wife's skirt and mounted straight away.

Five minutes later they both collapsed in a heap of satisfaction. The man pulled up his trousers and the wife returned to her scrubbing. Suddenly the man turned round and kicked his wife gently on the bum. "Ouch," she protested, "how can you do that when we've just had so much pleasure together?" "That," he retorted, "is for not turning round to see who it was!"

Lubrication

All this activity can become a trifle wearing. To avoid friction burns, you had better oil your loins.

A company boss was expecting to go home for a quiet birthday with his family. Then, just before it was time to leave, his desirable secretary asked him if he wanted to come back to her flat for a drink. Having fantasised for years about his secretary, he couldn't accept quick enough.

Back at the flat, they had a couple of drinks and then the secretary said she needed to go into her bedroom to 'see to a few things'. On her way she dimmed the lights and looked back with a smile on her face. The boss could stand it no longer. He took off all his clothes and rushed towards the bedroom door.

Just before he got there, the door burst open. "Happy birthday to you," sang his wife, children, work mates and several friends.

Getting Carried Away

A drop of the hard stuff can remove your inhibitions.
But take too much and you'll either fail to perform or
deserve an applause.

(Don't try this at home, children)

Daniel finally plucked up enough courage to ask his girlfriend to go to bed with him. She said 'yes' immediately, so Daniel thought they would have an enjoyable erotic evening. But, after an hour of hard work she was still showing no sign of enjoying herself.

"What's the matter?" he asked.
"It's your organ. I don't think it's big enough," she said.
"Well I didn't think I'd be playing in a Cathedral," he retorted.

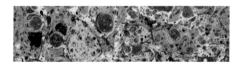

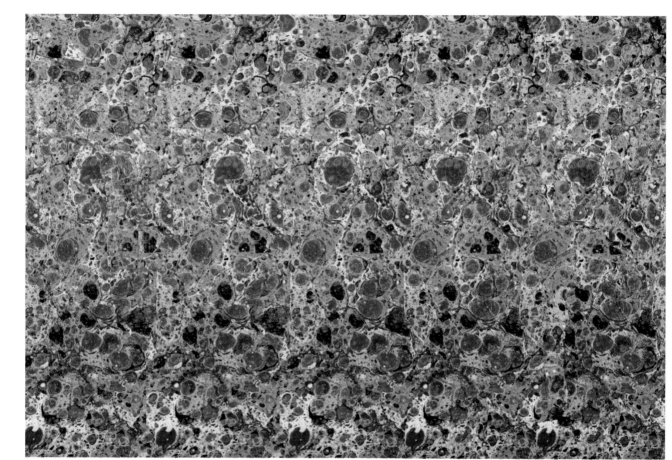

Two's Company

But ménage à trois is more exciting.

If you invite friends round to tea, make sure there is room for everybody to relax.

A young student was telling his friends about his new girlfriend. He was going on about how wonderful she was and what a lucky lad he would be if she would marry him.

"You can't be serious about marrying her though," said one of his friends. "She's slept with every one in Essex," added another.

The student thought about it a while and replied, "Essex isn't such a big place anyway."

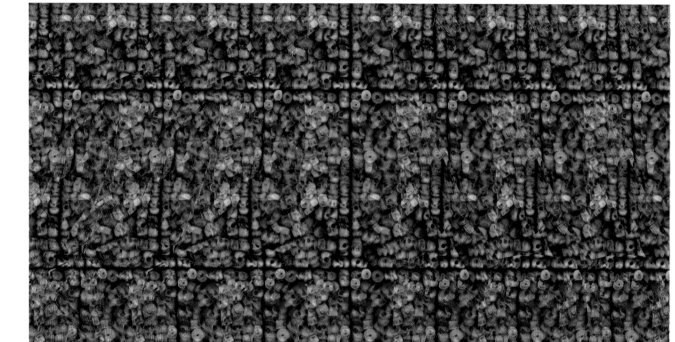

Take Care

Did you know that humans are the only species which procreate (that's posh for 'bonk') for recreation?

But nature didn't intend it that way. So watch out or you may end up like the last page.

An old man wandered into a brothel. Switching on his hearing aid, he asked the madam for a girl. "How old are you grandad?" said the madam. "Eighty-five," replied the old man.

"Eighty-five?" repeated the madam, "forget it, you've had it."

The old man looked a bit bemused and then reached for his wallet saying, "Then how much do I owe you?"

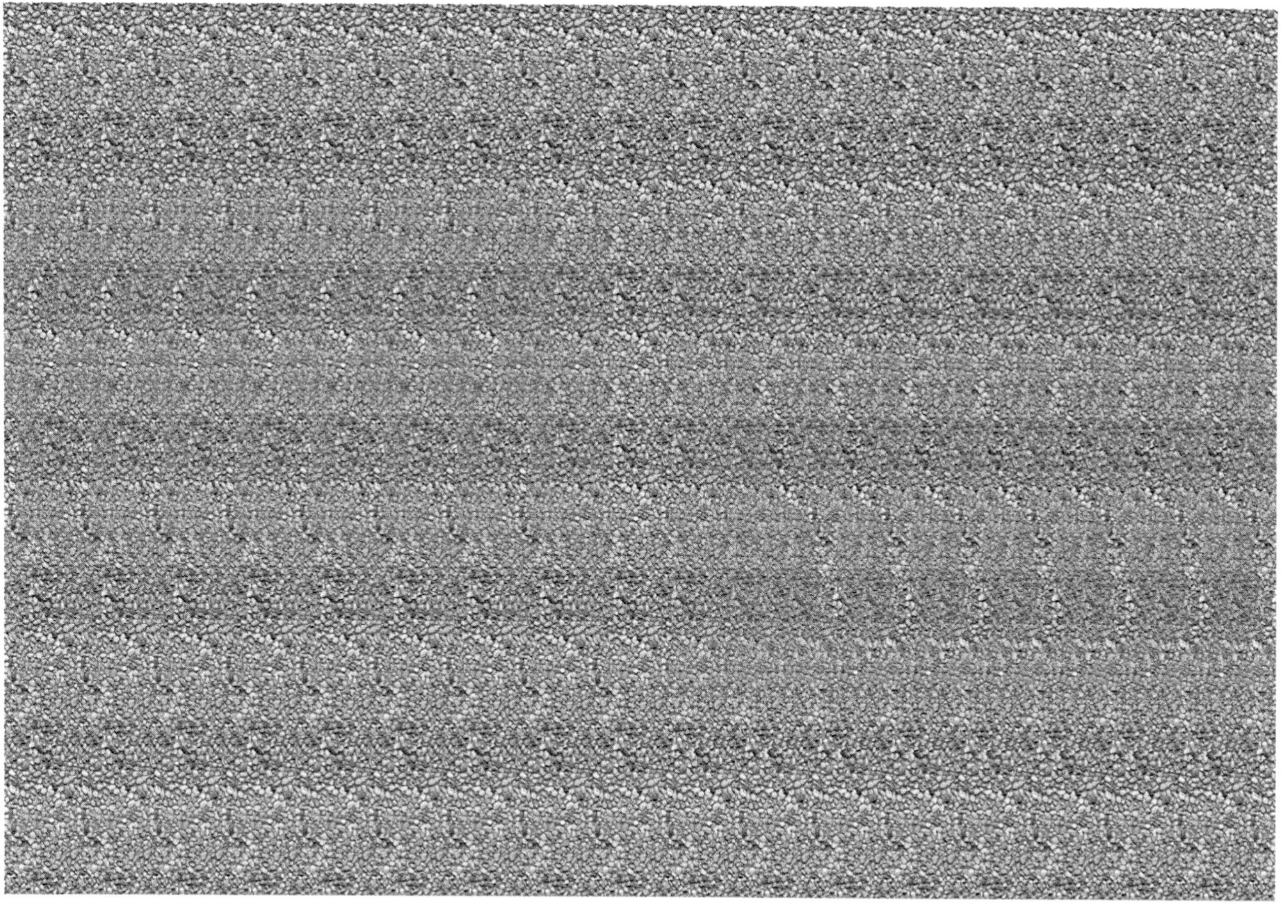

MORE HUMOUR TITLES...

Sex Trivia: The Bedside Guide

Does sex turn you on? Then here's a bedside companion that's titillating, weird, erotic, bizarre, sizzling, shocking, hilarious... and packed with thousands of TRUE FACTS! £3.99

The Bog Book

How much time do you spend in the bog every day? Letting valuable time go to waste? Not any longer! Fill your brain while you empty your bowels...*In the shape of a toilet seat* £3.99

The Hangover Handbook

Over 100 hangover remedies, an exclusive hangover ratings chart, a hangover clinic, etc., etc. *96* pages *In the shape of a beercan* £3.99

Down the Pan:
Amuse Yourself in the Toilet

An hilarious collection of cartoons, jokes and silly stories... great toilet accidents... famous toilets of history... even juggling toilet rolls. £3.99

Drinking Man's Survival Guide

Packed full of weird and wonderful ways to enjoy your drink... and survive to drink again another day! *BIG VALUE 200 pages* £3.99

Golf for The Girls

Some shred tips for the fair sex on the fairway. A wicked send up of this hallowed sport for the lone female entering the male dominated world of golf. £3.99

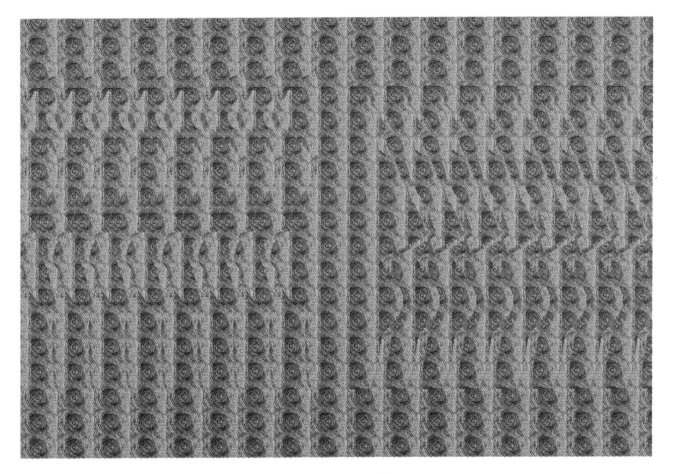

Whoops!!!